"White's eye for the details of everyday life shows that all of our existence is a miracle, if only we will pause long enough to notice. So, turn off your cell phone and allow On LIFE to speak to you, and you will be richly rewarded."
— Larry Dossey, MD, Author: *One Mind: How Our Individual Mind Is Part of a Greater Consciousness and Why It Matters*

"This is just the book we need to help us get through a difficult time. With wise advice for challenges large and small, Dr. White offers us hope when we need it the most."
— Mark C. Taylor, Columbia University, Author: *Seeing Silence*

"Reading On LIFE felt much like observing a flowing river on a summer day. The river is the same and yet different every moment. While reflecting something external, it's actually taking you within."
— Praveen Suthrum, Entrepreneur, Author: *Scope Forward*

"He challenges us to create our own life guidelines. Love this! Dr. White is a masterful teacher."
— Robyn Benson, Doctor of Oriental Medicine, Author: *Travel with Vitality: 7 Solutions for Sleeping Well, Staying Fit and Avoiding Illness*

"Welcome to my life! Dr. White has gracefully gathered a variety of timely topics to help us to be positive in life and comfortable in periods of change."
— P. David Poling, PhD, Author: *Sea of Glory: A Novel*

"Refreshing! A cardiologist addresses the important things in life – from the heart. Certain to be recommended reading for many of my patients!"

– Mimi Guarneri, MD, Author: *108 Pearls to Awaken Your Healing Potential*

"Let's not forget that no matter how fortunate, eventually we all face challenges which are universal to life. Create new direction on your journey with Dr. White's perfect life prescription."

– Sunil Pai, MD, Author: *An Inflammation Nation*

"In On LIFE and its accompanying workbook, Dr. White has written an essential, and may I say existential guidebook for living a life well lived. Truly a guide for us all!"

– Steven R. Gundry, MD, Author: *The Plant Paradox* and *The Longevity Paradox*

"With the vulnerability of sharing his own personal experiences, Dr. White emphasizes the everyday and leaves us feeling all the better about ourselves."

– Bill O'Neill, NM State Senator, Author: *The Freedom of the Ignored*

On LIFE

Thoughts on
Life's Challenges

Harvey J. White, MD
Guiding Conscious Living

VesselPRESS

100601 4th Street NW
Albuquerque, NM 87114
www.VesselPressPublishing.com
505-828-3000

First Paperback Edition: July 2020
Library of Congress Control Number: 2020907644
- ISBN's -
Book: 978-1-7348967-0-1
Mobi: 978-1-7348967-2-5
Epub: 978-1-7348967-3-2
Journal: 978-1-7348967-1-8

Cover and Interior Design by Diane Rigoli, www.RigoliCreative.com
Photography by Kip Malone

Table of Contents

Make a *DIFFERENCE*

Plan to make a difference today

    See the goal

    Not just another day

    Not the easy way

    Stand for something

Be bold, aim high, have spirit

Make a difference today

                      – HJW

Preface

A career in medicine is a curious experience. The naïve student starts the first day enthusiastic but nervous. Although conditioned by early life events, each student is being groomed to fill a vital role in society. The days are steeped in scientific learning. First, the healthy human body. How does it develop and how does it function? Next, illnesses. Names of conditions meant to confuse. The long days and nights of toil seem endless. Eventually, graduation, followed by many years of supervised practical experience—the modern-day apprenticeship.

The outcome is an "expert," likely still naïve to the greater world, but poised to contribute and fill the role imbued with the seriousness of the title "Doctor of Medicine."

It is only then that the real learning begins. It is only then that responsibility begins to weather and shape the person. It is only then that daily interaction with patients begins to educate the doctor's soul.

And the process takes years. Along the way the physician endures the challenges of his or her own life experiences. And finally, after decades of being a student of life as well as medicine, the mature physician emerges.

Being a doctor is far more than mastering the skills evolved from a continually expanding fund of knowledge. The great physician is a guardian of living. He or she, in the final analysis, is trusted with helping each patient navigate the journey of their lives.

And that is a humbling realization. For the real learning comes not from books or journals, but from those individuals my colleagues and

I care for. We are considered experts, but the real heroes are more often the patients and their families.

The essays highlighted in this book are the harvest of the decades of my experience, both inside and outside of medical centers. They are the yield of the observation and processing of human behavior, including my own, and the product of studying how we all approach some of life's most common challenges and how they are overcome. These are ingredients for a successful life—one of vitality and abundance.

Never easy, but forever possible.

Harvey J. White, MD
Albuquerque
January 2020

Introduction

The world is enthralled with hero medicine: vaccinations for just about everything, transplants to save a rare life, genetic splicing to ensure a disease-free future. The daily news is infiltrated with such seeming miracles.

But it's important to keep such heroics in perspective. It may not be the complex and the dramatic that truly enhance human health but rather the simple. We have indeed found that how we live—how we think, move, and nourish our bodies—has far more influence on our longevity and happiness than the latest cure.

How to live a conscious and effective life has been embedded in civilizations' teachings for millennia. The proverbs of the Bible, the teachings of Confucius, the maxims of Hammurabi. But the simple often gets lost along the way and doesn't become apparent until we mature through our life experience.

Sorted into twenty-five concise topics covering many of life's challenges, this book sheds light on the simple—especially on how we think. And in so doing it reveals how the simple can be so profound. Without being too dogmatic, it suggests some solutions to assist us in overcoming the barriers that these challenges pose.

Starting appropriately with the topic "On BEGINNING," this book aims to help us take a step forward and not wallow in complacency. It ends with "On TRAVEL," not to focus on leisure, but to encourage us to explore the world around us and to grow from planning along the way.

An accompanying workbook—designed in a journal style—helps to bring these lessons to bear on our lives. Each topic includes challenging questions and suggested commitments that spur us to think more deeply about the lesson and how we can change our attitudes if necessary.

Living is not easy. One should not be embarrassed to admit defeat at times or to experience a sense of being overwhelmed. But each of us, even in our most difficult times, has great potential. Read on to discover and better understand that potential.

On BEGINNING

I Am in the Game

BEGINNING CAN BE CHALLENGING. THE START OF SOMETHING NEW. Think back to that first day at a new school. All seemed big and overwhelming. Unknown hallways, foreign faces, and imposing teachers. Little familiar—except that feeling of intense insecurity.

"This is not safe."

"I wish I was back in my old school."

"If only I knew someone!"

For many, this feeling is all too familiar and echoes through many of life's transitions. It is certainly a common feeling with any new beginning.

Beginning, however, is a recurrent theme in our lives.

Boarding that plane to fly overseas, the first day at camp, opening night of a performance, a new hair-style—each brings with it the new and unknown. Each is a step onto unstable ground. But most transitions, and the new beginnings they bring, are unavoidable as we navigate the byways of life.

So, how do we handle these testing transitions?

Curiously, beginning can be threatening to some and yet an adventure to others. From a distance it would seem that many of our friends and acquaintances weather life's transitions with ease and appear to make changes with little forethought. Most of us, however, approach challenging changes with at least a bit of trepidation.

How we approach transitions, new beginnings in life, can be defeating or empowering. Rather than choosing stasis, or even retreat, consider the energy derived from taking that fork in the road with a lightness of step, from choosing rebirth over crisis.

Consider three attitudes that may grease the wheels of change:

- **Acceptance:** Change is inevitable. Even grand transitions such as birth and death are beyond our control. "I don't want to grow up" is not a choice. Acceptance will soothe the anxiety while it prepares us for the natural unfolding of life.

- **Excitement:** A new beginning often takes us into the unknown. Think of life as an exploration. From birth, each of us is an explorer. Whether we're changing careers or searching for new species or even galaxies, a fresh start can be exciting!

- **Choice:** Choice is amazingly powerful. When we choose, we reinforce our being, our singular presence in life. We make our mark and may indirectly tap into a force much grander than ourselves. If nothing else, choosing to take a step in a new direction puts us in touch with ourselves.

These simple ways of seeing the renewal of beginning often yield a profound sense of self—present, alive, and intent. The challenge to each of us is to keep growing.

Trying a new food, traveling to a foreign land, developing a new habit—all are examples of new beginnings that imply:

I am in the game!

On CHANGE

All will be OK!

IT WAS TIME FOR ME TO BUY A NEW TRUCK. THE PICKUP HAD reliably hauled horses and performed farm chores for almost fifteen years, with many a battle scar to show for it.

It was time. A pragmatic, utilitarian decision. But was I ready? Like holding on to an old pair of running shoes, I had gotten used to that truck, and in truth I was not emotionally ready. To make things harder, like all new vehicles, trucks had evolved dramatically over that decade and a half. Electronic everything! But no cassette player!

I am still working through that transition because I, like many, have difficulty with change.

Whether it is giving up that old vehicle, those comfortable shoes, a familiar apartment, a well-worn jacket, scratched sunglasses, or any of the numerous belongings we encircle ourselves with, parting can be difficult. And what of involuntary change in our surroundings—change we have little or no control over? A new stoplight on the drive to work, a fence separating a neighboring field, a building where once there was a view—each requires adaptation. Advance to more profound change such as loss of one's health, or perhaps the deeper loss embedded in parting with a friend or loved one. These monumental changes make parting with an old truck seem trivial.

What is it that makes change challenging?

Are the difficulties age related?

How do we cope with change?

And how do we prepare for the ultimate change—our own death?

The challenges of change are many—some simple and some complex. We get comfortable. Do new shoes ever feel like the ones we're discarding? We get complacent. Is a new diet easy to start? We covet the familiar. How will I ever remember this new password? It all seems overwhelming.

But these challenges are trivial. Ultimately, change threatens our very presence. Not only is all this impermanent, but so too are we! Now that is hard to embrace. In fact, are not all the changes we endure just symbolic of the truth that nothing is permanent?

As we grow older, change becomes even more problematic. Consider the changes our parents or grandparents as members of the "greatest generation" experienced: radio, TV, microwaves, refrigerators, computers, airplanes, rockets, space walks, nuclear bombs, nylon, rayon, and of course plastic—along with another new phone to learn. Wow! Nothing permanent.

As we age our flexibility vanishes. We lose plasticity—not simply physically but mentally as well. Our habits become security as our capacity to learn new algorithms in life declines. Life's truths become fewer but clearer. And as we approach the end, all seems to tunnel in. Yes, change becomes more challenging as we age. That is natural and acceptable.

But even as we grow older, perhaps there are ways to cope with change that improve its palatability—and even make it fun!

- **Accept:** Change is inevitable, and the sooner that is recognized, the easier life's transitions become. Acceptance, however, requires a certain attitude—not simply giving in, not simply caving, and certainly not resisting. Resisting change is erosive to the spirit. It traps one in a negative space. Grace, harmony, equanimity, and peace all imply acceptance and ease resistance.

- **Create:** Change that we create, that we induce, that we design and execute, is far more acceptable. Being proactive instead of reactive. What do we want? Where do we go? Not the passenger in the car but the driver, establishing goals and making decisions. A sense of self is preserved.

Even our own passing can in some sense be managed. Although challenging to consider, making decisions about death can be empowering. Choosing a final resting place, picking music, designing a headstone, writing a poem—all are activities that leave one with a sense of engagement or participation.

And finally, there's the antidote of recognizing we have lived fully. That can only happen if we live a considered life. Does it have meaning? Does it contribute to humanity? Is it satisfying? For without those qualities an emptiness will escort us to death.

Change is inevitable. The universe unfolds. We change. The end will come.

All will be OK!

On DECISION

Have No Regrets

DECISIONS ARE A CONSTANT IN EACH OF OUR LIVES—CRUCIAL WAY
points as we navigate our days and life's larger voyage. Consider the
many decisions we make daily:

What to wear in the morning.

What to choose from the items on a menu.

Which route to take home from work to avoid congested traffic.

Those are the easy ones—almost routine and rarely stressful. Yet we
all are constantly faced with choices that we just can't seem to move
through—decisions that hang over us and seem so difficult to resolve:

Should I leave my job for another?

Should I commit to this relationship in spite of its issues?

Is it time to seek a doctor's attention for my hoarse voice?

We have all confronted a decision that yields little but procrastination. A choice we see no simple solution for. Why is it that some
decisions come so easily while others appear monumental? What are
some of the characteristics of those looming decisions that keep us
paralyzed? And how can we break through to a freed-up future?

A decision that leaves us confounded often has one or more qualities
that lend themselves to stalemate:

The available options appear of equal value.

Each option has a strong upside.

Each is fraught with problems.

Choosing implies a sense of loss.

We fear the possible consequences.

Yes, decisions are often difficult when there doesn't appear to be a clear winner. It is remarkably easy to become paralyzed.

So, how does one approach the challenge and come out a victor?

Some solutions are both simple and profound:

- **Awareness**: Awakening to life and being aware is an integral part of conscious living. Decision is a cornerstone and begins with being aware of our circumstances and acknowledging that we have a decision to make, an opportunity to embrace. We need to avoid ignorance, because we have no one to blame but ourselves. Wake up and pay attention, and decision will come more easily. Awareness is the first step.

- **Action**: Action has power. Inaction is erosive. Rejecting indecision and embracing decision generates motion. "Yes, I did it" captures the outcome. What a great feeling! It is often far better for one's self-worth to make a decision and move on. And grasping the moment and garnering that internal reinforcement of confidence often outstrips any concern about making the wrong decision.

- **Acceptance**: Curiously, there is rarely a conscious decision in life that is ruinous. Few result in irreversible error. And accepting decision as an unavoidable part of life's journey certainly eases any distasteful result. When we recognize that there is no single right path, decision becomes easier. Accept all outcomes.

Making a difficult decision can create disabling anxiety. But decision is often unavoidable, and indecision is no solution. Regrettably, without our active engagement, decisions will often be made for us—one way or another. Be bold and break the logjam. Be aware, take action, and accept the outcome.

Have no regrets!

On GREATNESS

Reach For It

"THAT WAS A GREAT PLAY."

"What a great job!"

"It was great to see you."

"He did great."

"Great" is one of those words with multiple meanings—depending on the context. Often it implies a superlative outcome or result. Commonly we use it to describe another person. But what does it mean when we apply "great" to our own activities? Can we use it to set a high bar for our goals? What would it be like to ascribe greatness to ourselves?

The statement "I'm going to be a great person" may sound egotistical, and yet how empowering!

"I will do great things!"

Great things—those that are impactful, memorable, lasting, consequential, meaningful, rewarding.

The common conception of greatness may seem beyond the reach of many. But a goal of greatness has the potential of lifting us up and setting us on a trajectory of both enhanced personal fulfilment and enhanced contribution to family and community.

Being great does not require fame. It does not require going down in the annals of history. Rather, being great or doing great things requires a state of mind. How do we get there? Here are some steps toward success:

- Define your goal, where you want to go

- Outline the steps required on the journey

- Acknowledge when you have arrived

- Set a reward for self-recognition

Certainly we cannot become great, even if only in our own mind, without a goal. World-class athletes, artists, authors, and the like all seem to define their goals early in life. Rarely do they simply fall into success. Theirs results from clarity of outcome and the desire to get there.

That desire is often broken down into steps. In the early nineteenth century several iconic individuals in the fields of medicine and the arts made difficult journeys to Paris to advance their learning and skills. Each knew that such a journey was a prerequisite to greatness. In their day apprenticeships served a similar purpose, often with significant sacrifice. The journey to greatness may require going back to school, moving, finding the right mentor, carving out personal time, or even enduring financial hardship. And of course, practice, practice, practice!

Do we ever really arrive? In certain instances, yes. Completing each step toward a goal, and especially acknowledging when the journey is near completion, is important because then a sense of satisfaction can arise. On the contrary, never feeling fulfilled is corrosive and unsettling and can discourage you from continuing on the path to your goals. Admit to yourself when you have "made it."

And when you've arrived, consider a reward. A break? A party? A vacation? Self-congratulations and pleasure followed perhaps—then and only then—by a new goal, another manifestation of greatness.

Striving to be great, although often beneficial to others and humanity, is in essence a personal quest. Personal validation, confirmation of capability, and assertion of our very existence—in this place, at this point in time—are at the core. For it is not what others think of us but what we think of ourselves that counts.

Reach for it.

On CREATIVITY

Be Inspired

MOST OF US WHO HAVE REACHED OUR ADULT YEARS TEND TO avoid creative exploits. We consider ourselves not good enough. Art, music, design, writing are all the domains of the other guy. Or perhaps the playgrounds of youth, distant from our current lives. To even approach the subject of creativity may seem daunting and out of bounds.

And yet creativity is the hallmark of humanity. Only we as humans have the capacity to create consciously. Not to simply discover, not to simply uncover, but to truly imagine and export something from our minds into reality. Perhaps artificial intelligence, crafted in the likeness of the human mind, will have such capacity in the future, but until then the responsibility is ours and ours alone.

And what a mystery it is to transform the once unimagined into reality, to go from nothingness to something, to spring from a nebulous impulse to near permanence.

So...

What is creativity?

Is it latent in all of us?

How can it be fostered?

And what does it say about our existence?

Creativity is foremost an exercise of the mind. It is the spark of an idea, self-generated in an individual's thought, which ignites a transformation from nothingness to life. An impulse to write a new piece of music. The drive to write a poem. The desire to craft a new art form. These are the classics. But creativity is more, and it doesn't need to be outstanding and certainly not public. The gardener arranges her planting; the homeless person builds a new shelter.

Each of these activities springs from our minds. In each we create a new reality. For icons like Leonardo da Vinci, it appeared almost preordained. But creativity lies within us all. We all have the power to think beyond our immediate circumstance, to imagine, to dream. And we all have the capacity to transform those ideas into reality.

Unquestionably creativity can be fostered. Recent studies support the long-held precepts that living with less structure, and living on the edge in stressed conditions, may have helped artists discover unfound ideas and cultivate the creative process. Stepping outside our comfort zone may, however, just entail doing something different like reading a provocative article. Recognizing this desire to create has even spawned teaching opportunities, as in a local art studio that introduces painting to the uninitiated. Whether self-generated or stimulated by others, we all deserve to grow as creative beings.

Humans don't have to lead lives of monotonous repetition. In fact, the history of humanity has witnessed the never-ending pursuit of the new. We constantly look to the future. And that future will forever be shaped by our desires and capacity to create.

Be inspired.

On FOCUS

Tune In

THINK OF YOUR LAST VACATION—PERHAPS A DRIVING TRIP WITH family or a friend. New sights, new sounds, new experiences.

Are the memories crisp and clear? Do parts of the trip seem "just like yesterday"? Why is such an experience so vivid?

"The first time we had been to the Rockies." The novelty and newness of it all may certainly be a factor. But perhaps there's more to that clarity of moment than simply a fresh experience. Perhaps it is in the clarity of the mind. Perhaps it is in the mind's focus—that capacity to see things clearly and to experience and enjoy each moment—uncluttered by all the usual daily distractions. "I have rarely felt so alive!"

In contrast, our day-in-and-day-out existence is often unfocused. We push ourselves to multitask and perhaps mindlessly go through our daily routines:

Morning stretch

Catch up on email

Check the weather and traffic

Coffee on the commute

Multiple meetings to start the day

On the road visiting clients

Texts from family

Workout and shopping on the way home

Grill out

CNN

Netflix

Shower

News on the phone

Repeat

All good, but potentially haphazard and numbing. What have we really accomplished? Have we made meaningful connections? Have we moved forward on our life's mission? Likely not. Getting the most out of life requires some degree of focus, bringing our mind to bear on certain core elements. These don't have to be career related, but may be commitments, hobbies, charities, or even adventures.

How can we gain that focus? Here are some suggestions:

- **Slow down**: Our days may seem a whirlwind. And yet life's pace can be controlled. In spite of so many outside distractions and demands, the choice is really ours. Breathe.

- **Prioritize**: At times we seem to be trying to be all things to all people. Instead, we need to make choices. Narrowing our efforts and energies to the most meaningful and critical endeavors can reap great rewards—and great memories.

- **Set goals**: Without goals, our days are random. One idea is to write a personal mission statement. What is my purpose? What do I need to focus on to make it a reality? Goals intensify our focus.

Life goes by far too fast as it is. Like the view out of a speeding train window, our lives can often be a blur. What do we really see? Do we really have clear and vivid memories? Perhaps life would be more rewarding and clearer if we focused more—slowing down, setting some personal goals, and prioritizing our daily activities. Taking time to "smell the roses" may not be such a farfetched idea after all.

Tune in.

On CIRCUMSTANCE

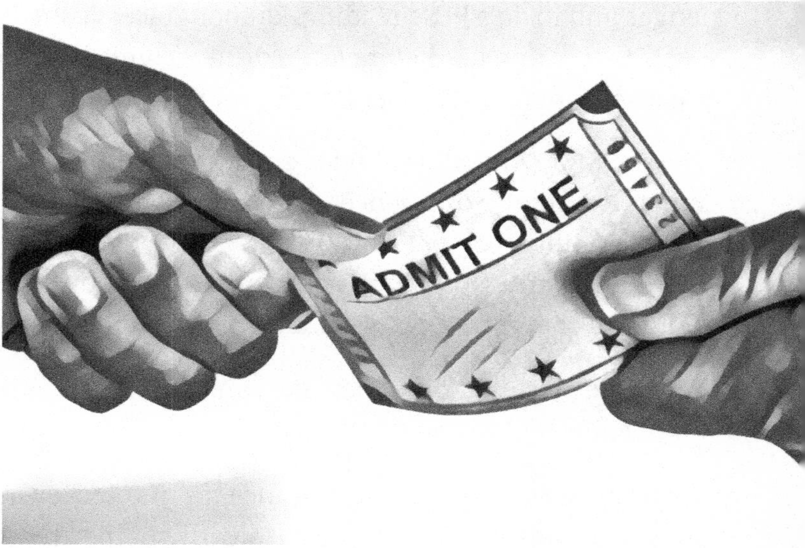
ADMIT ONE

See the Opportunity

MY EARLY MORNING IN A LOCAL COFFEE SHOP WAS NATURALLY quiet, allowing me a moment to contemplate the day's work challenges and to do a little reading. Random faces rushed in and dashed out after picking up their favorite drink to ignite the morning. Barely a pause from the customers, aside from a few retirees in the corner.

The next day I had a ten o'clock appointment in the same location. What a dramatic difference. All were lingering—groups of friends and acquaintances, both inside and out. Dynamic conversations, intense and earnest. Several acquaintances came to our table to say hello and chat for a bit. A veritable mid-morning social hour.

The same place, but different times and different circumstances. And totally different experiences.

We often seem to take circumstance for granted, even though it asserts a powerful influence in our lives, whether recognized or not. Because of this influence, perhaps we should give it more respect.

What actually is circumstance?

Is circumstance random?

Can we design circumstances?

Can we make circumstances work to our advantage?

Circumstance is that immediate condition we find ourselves in. It is the environment, the context, the situation of our current experience. It can be subtle when you're in quiet surroundings, distracting when with a crying infant, or disturbing when in the chaos of boarding an airplane. Social moments, such as one-on-one intimate conversations, contrast sharply with the noise of screaming fans in a soccer stadium.

Often we think of circumstances as being entirely random, and some in fact are. We arrive at the coffee shop and find it closed because they have a flooded kitchen. We attend a party thinking we won't know anyone, only to find an old friend and enjoy an evening of reminiscence. We board a plane and are seated next to a famous musician and get tickets to her next concert. Who would have thought?

And yet circumstance is not entirely a chance occurrence. We can influence our circumstances—more than we may wish. Often, we may not really want to take responsibility for the conditions we find ourselves in. Yet we do have the power to design our circumstances. Moving to Hollywood to pursue a passion for becoming a movie star may seem hopelessly romantic, but there is no better path. Or perhaps shadowing a surgeon in hopes of getting a strong medical school recommendation, or regularly attending a networking event in pursuit of prospective clients.

Putting ourselves in an opportunistic circumstance can work to our advantage. But having a predetermined goal can certainly accelerate the outcome. So a desire to become a budding artist may be advantaged by researching the best schools for artists in New York City, or by simply moving to Montmartre in Paris.

Thinking about how circumstance can work to our benefit can be uplifting and personally energizing. Call it circumstance by design.

See the opportunity.

On HEALTH

I Had That Once!

A FELLOW STRUGGLING WITH ARTHRITIS MET WITH AN OLD acquaintance, Jim. After a few idle comments, the conversation turned to health, and the fellow soon posed a question: "Jim, have you ever had arthritis?" Jim frowned, pondered the question, pursed his lips, and stated emphatically, "I had that once!"

What is it about health that is so consuming to one individual and seemingly a nonissue for another?

Are some people and families simply cursed with health concerns?

Why is our healthcare system so monumental in scale?

And can we as individuals and as a society significantly stem the health challenges we currently confront?

These sorts of questions can be distilled down to just two:

Can I be healthier?

What can I do to minimize the impact when I am not well?

Each of these questions can be answered in a positive and constructive fashion, and the lessons may be pertinent to society at large.

Yes, we can all be healthier! And so much revolves around how we think and how we approach life.

- **Be disciplined**: Always easier said than done, being disciplined offers countless benefits in our life—whether in saying "good morning" to our workmates, limiting food at each meal, or enjoying a noontime walk. Having control over our impulses and being disciplined about forming healthful habits yield bountiful returns.

- **Be involved**: Applying oneself, whether at work or home, limits self-absorption and creates a healthy mindset and outlook. A sense of accomplishment can be a powerful antidote to most any health challenge.

- **Remain curious**: A youthful interest in our surroundings draws us into exploring the world with a fresh and curious mind. The world looks brighter!

- **Stay active**: In the equine world, the old adage "motion creates lotion" is key to a healthy horse. We are no different.

- **Optimize relationships**: Interacting with others keeps us from excessive inward focus. Any sense of being alone with one's health worries will fade.

- **Help others**: Giving perhaps does more for the soul than any other act and creates a sense of self-worth. A win-win endeavor for all!

In other words, live fully! You'll be astonished at how much healthier you feel.

These same suggestions serve as answers for the question of how to minimize the downside of any illness. "I am too busy to get sick." "I have too much to do." "I am not done living." At the very least those attitudes will make an illness more tolerable and may in fact diminish its impact and shorten its duration.

Indeed, how we think—our attitudes—are profoundly impactful.

Our healthcare system is overwhelmed. Heart disease continues to flourish, diabetes is rampant, and dementia is now the next frontier. What is it that generates such illness? Arguably, our "western" way of living is the cause. Daily stress, lack of meaning, poor habits, malnourishing foods, and sedentary living yield a petri dish of ill health. It is clear we will never win the "fix-it game." Success revolves around the "prevention game." So much harkens back to personal responsibility. It is incumbent on each of us to have the desire to be as healthy as possible and take the necessary steps to get there. The alternative is the "losing game," both for ourselves and society.

Not so apparent when we are young, there is truth to the adage that health is everything. Whether we like it or not, we do have significant control over our own health—a responsibility that none should avoid. And if ill, we can certainly limit its consequences.

So the next time you feel arthritic, or whatever, remember Jim and his maxim:

"I had that once!"

On LIGHT

Turn the Lights On

A GRANDSON WAS ASKED TO GO OVER TO HIS GRANDFATHER'S TO once again help him with organizing some bills. They were scattered on the kitchen counter in a bit of disarray. And just after "Hi, Grandpa," his grandfather said, "Turn the lights on so you can see what you are doing."

Light. So vital to our existence, so taken for granted.

What was the young man's grandfather really saying?

Is light simply a utility?

How does light affect our moods?

Does light claim more meaning as we age?

Grandpa's comment about turning the lights on is perhaps more profound than its face value. Yes, turning on a light would permit the grandson to better see the papers before him. But like the eyes of many young people, his were probably sharp, and he could have done the organizing even in a dimly lit room. Perhaps the grandfather was admitting his infirmity, recognizing that he could no longer do this ordinary task, that he needed more light in the form of personal capacity. Perhaps the light symbolized youth for Gramps. And for many, light may symbolize life, something that the grandfather knew was passing.

Light is much more than a simple utility that allows us to navigate our planet. Light generated by the sun fuels life itself, from complex plant growth and photosynthesis, to seasonal changes and hormonal cycles. But even these more profound utilities pale in comparison to the symbolism that light conveys. Throughout the history of humanity, light has symbolized life, and darkness death. Light also symbolizes knowledge as in the old adage "turn the lights on," meaning, wake up and pay attention. So in spite of all the artificial light humans now shower on the planet, the symbolic importance of light persists.

Beyond the symbolic, light, or lack of it, profoundly affects our moods. In broad terms, light generates energy, enthusiasm, willingness, and hope. In more subtle terms, pale light is conducive to tranquility; soft light, to harmony; bright light, to alertness; and blazing light, to agitation. Without light, however, our energy turns low and eventually dissipates. Light in all forms is vital to our very existence.

And as we age, it seems that the importance of light is amplified. Rarely do we find a dimly lit nursing home. Rarely an older person in front of the TV without the lights on. Rarely an older person who is a night owl. Contrast that with the teenager who seems to never go to bed early, and sleeps until noon. With age, we awaken with the sun.

Light is to be appreciated, and even treasured, but never wasted.

So, when you just can't seem to find your way, or you're having a hard moment in life, remember, you can always...

Turn the lights on.

On HABITS

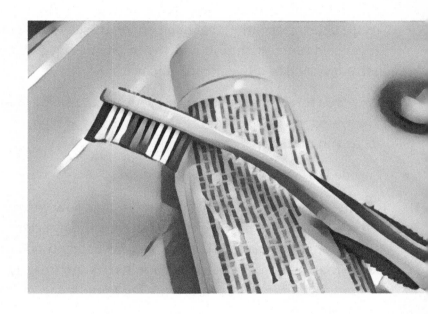

Decide—Today, Easy, Daily

A WHILE AGO I MADE A CHANGE IN MY BREAKFAST SCHEDULE, AND it seems to be working! Mondays, a protein smoothie (more on the recipe below), repeating that habit on Wednesdays and Fridays. Low-sugar cold cereal with fruit and yogurt on Tuesdays, Thursdays, and Saturdays, and finally, eggs on Sundays.

Wow, you might think, this guy is overly compulsive. I, like many, had discovered my blood sugar on a lab test to be too high, so I needed to focus and make some changes.

I needed to look at my habits.

Our lifestyle—how we think and process life, how we eat and nourish our bodies, and how we move and remain physically fit—serves as the foundation of our health. And our habits function like steel rebar that reinforces concrete. Some habits are healthy, providing strength. Others are erosive, leaving our foundations prone to cracks and crumbles.

Smoking, a progressively less common habit in America, stands as a great example of a habit that undermines our foundations and leaves us weakened and vulnerable.

Contrast that with regular exercise, a foundation reinforcement leaving us solid and resilient.

Though easily understood, many do not have the attitude necessary to succeed at forming new habits. "I tried that before and failed." "I have no time." "I don't really like to do that." "I'm too old." "I'm tired." "I can't."

Heard any of those lines before—from others, or possibly even yourself?

Perhaps it's not all that difficult. Perhaps failure is not a foregone conclusion. So, what might be some ingredients for success? How can we more readily transform our habits?

- **Decision**: All change in life starts with motivation—and a decision. One must decide: "I can't keep living like this. I have had enough. I'm done with this. I see a better future. And I am ready." So, decide!

- **Today**: Start today, not tomorrow, and especially not next week. There is no time like now. A decision deserves implementation. If you wait, you may wait forever!

- **Easy**: The easier the habit the more likely it will be implemented. If too difficult, habits simply serve as a target for procrastination. My protein smoothie is the easy version. Done in a shaker bottle (no electric blender to wash), the smoothie includes some water, two scoops of vegetable-based protein powder, a scoop of powdered greens, a probiotic, six ounces of kefir, and six ounces of almond milk along with a dash of hemp seeds. Down the hatch!

- **Daily**: Optimal habits are regular. And a daily or twice daily schedule is most likely to secure success. Brushing one's teeth, which a century ago was a rare phenomenon, is now a habit that most practice regularly.

Embracing a decision, starting today, choosing an easy course, and committing to a daily routine—all spell success. But even these tips are not a guarantee. That is why I have occasionally turned to a chart to track my habits. Monday through Sunday across the top and my list of important habits down the left side. I simply check off my accomplishments as the day proceeds. Morning stretching, breakfast as outlined, greetings to all my co-workers, 10:00 calisthenics, 12:00 rapid walk, 3:00 snack, and onward. It works (for the most part), and it might for you!

Health is not a foregone conclusion. Creating and maintaining health requires a strong focus on how we live—our thinking, eating, and moving. These fundamental elements of our lifestyle serve as the foundation of our health. Reinforce them with effective habits, and don't look back.

Decide—today, easy, and daily!

On INNER
STRENGTH

Be That Person

THE STOCK MARKET IS DOWN, DAUGHTER BETH IS ILL, CO-WORKER Mary did not show up for work, and your spouse forgot your anniversary. The world is a challenging place, and it seems we are constantly confronted by its vicissitudes. Staying strong in those times is far from easy. Unfortunately, we cannot dependably rely on others to boost us. Much requires inner strength.

Inner strength is a human characteristic that permits us to weather the moment and move forward on our own terms. Optimally, inner strength is self-generated. It is internally fueled by the spirit that lies within each of us. Only then can it exist and endure independently from surroundings and circumstances.

"Inner strength" is subtly different from "resilience." Resilience is defensive. It suggests a response to challenges and threats in life and implies a certain hardening or resistance to the elements. The resilient person is strong and can weather much. Inner strength, however, implies a burning furnace, an inner glow, a flame that penetrates and projects outward and forward. It is the quality of a leader and the person who not only reacts to change but creates it as well.

Is inner strength inherent?

Can it be taught?

Can it be cultivated?

On the surface it would seem that some just have it. Explorers on lonely treks and sailors who circumnavigate the globe stand out for their courage. Even the most self-confident individuals probably work to reinforce that trait. And admittedly, in this modern era, many are never really alone. Often a support team encourages them forward—one way or another. But they have the juice, often arrived at through observation and modeling someone they look up to.

Our lives are frequented with role models who teach us resolve. Looking back, some may choose their father or mother for their exemplary focus and self-sacrifice. In certain cultures, coming-of-age ceremonies accelerate the teaching of confidence and adaptability. A series of test situations was common in certain Native America tribes, often intended to cultivate the inner strength of a warrior spirit. Unfortunately, in contemporary society, inner strength is rarely directly taught.

For most of us, inner strength must be nurtured.

For those of us who see ourselves as a more common type of person—never to be left alone on an arctic ice sheet—what are some ingredients that may contribute to inner strength?

- **Self-awareness**: Continually reflecting on our own personal goals and position in life builds character. And avoiding comparing ourselves to others limits negative self-talk.

- **Self-evaluation**: Completing an inventory of our strengths and accepting ourselves completely reinforces self-appreciation and a sense of inner resolve.

- **Personal discipline**: Holding ourselves accountable contributes to a sense of accomplishment and adds strength to the fibers of our character.

- **Curiosity**: The desire to explore allows each of us to consciously observe the world through our own senses, generating a sense of being alive.

- **Contribution**: Giving to others not only nurtures them, but nurtures ourselves. Positive beliefs are reinforced, and a sense of self-worth is generated.

- **Contemplation**: Spending time alone for reflection may initially create agitation, but with time an inner peace accrues. Documenting one's thoughts and feelings can accelerate that process. We all deserve to set aside time to pause, contemplate our circumstances, and bolster our resolve to follow our life's purpose.

The value of inner strength cannot be overemphasized. An individual who masters this trait is not only more settled personally but can more confidently give to others and to society. Arguably, in life's journey this goal of increasing inner strength may stand out as one of the most important—the ultimate reward being a sense of peace as our life nears completion.

Be that person.

On BELIEF

Believe—or Not!

"I BELIEVE YOU."

I trust you, I am confident in you, I honor you, I have faith in you.

"I believe in an afterlife."

I trust, I am confident, I honor, I have faith.

We humans have an amazing capacity to believe and hold beliefs.

Beliefs are broad: belief in another, belief in a higher power, belief in a parent, belief in a principle, belief in a team, belief in a concept, belief in the future, belief in oneself!

What is belief?

Where does it come from?

Is it a mystery?

Is it immutable?

Belief is profound, and even a bit mysterious. Belief appears to be a process where we give permission to someone or something beyond our control to provide meaning and have responsibility in our lives. It is the result of letting go of what we self-manage and giving power to something beyond us. In believing, we extend ourselves beyond our immediate limits. We give over to the other.

As we mature, the creation of belief is a self-generated activity. It comes from us and us alone. We allow it to happen. Some would argue that certain beliefs come through a calling, a message, or an epiphany. But isn't it the case that even the most deeply held belief stems from personal experience? It is our experience that can permit a belief and also undermine it. Our experience allows us to trust, to have confidence, to honor, and to have faith—or not.

That is not to say there isn't mystery behind some beliefs. They may seem to come from nowhere. And yet even the most profound belief is often derived from our circumstances. We trust our parents early on because they are our entire world and we must do so to feel safe. We have confidence in our workmates due to their impeccable work ethic. We honor our Constitution because it seems to work—most of the time. And we have faith due to a certain mindset based on our experiences and what we've been exposed to.

The tenuous grounding of belief in personal experience results in the shocking reality that belief is not immutable. It is in fact conditional. Belief can change. A parent may fail us, a workmate turn corrupt, a team become less tight-knit, and the weather not be as predicted. People change teams, they switch channels, and they change religions.

And they can do this because belief is a self-generated mindset. We give ourselves permission to believe, and we can take it away.

Is that for naught? Is believing, then, a waste of time? Absolutely not, because beliefs serve as guideposts as we navigate life. They give us direction and provide meaning. They orient us. They permit us not to be in control of everyone and everything.

But what about the ultimate belief that seems immutable—belief in something cosmically bigger than humankind and the world as we know it? The Tao, God, Yahweh, Nature, Dark Matter...

For those who have that ultimate belief, its meaning is firm. And to them, maintaining such belief is essential and should not be questioned. And yet many live their lives with no such belief. We exist therefore we are—and there is nothing more. Theirs is simply a different belief.

One way of believing is not better than another. Unless to the detriment of others, there is no right way to believe. Belief is only that—a belief.

Believe—or not!

On ENOUGH

I've Had Just Enough

HOW OFTEN HAVE WE HEARD THE PHRASE "ENOUGH IS ENOUGH"? A sense of exasperation:

"I have had it!"

"I am at my limit!"

"We're done!"

"We've gone too far!"

All imply a sense of being over the top. But perhaps the concept of enough can be thought of more productively. Perhaps "enough" can be tamed and used to our advantage.

Can "enough" be considered in a positive light?

Can we use "enough" constructively in our lives?

How does one control "enough" and put it to good use?

While at a restaurant, one of the people at your table samples the hors d'oeuvres, has a large salad, eats several rolls, and devours his steak dinner with sides of potatoes and a vegetable medley. Dessert is on the way. Pushing back his chair he exclaims, "I think I have had enough!"

Another person at the table samples the appetizers, skips the salad, and asks for a "to go" box when her entrée arrives. She portions out a bit ahead of eating. She too enjoys the dinner and at the end remarks, "I think I have had just enough."

What a difference.

One person eats to excess, the other to moderation.

Consider "enough" in a positive light. In the first example, the situation gets out of hand for the diner and indicates little sense of control. The second diner exemplifies the self-control of an individual who knows her limits and easily manages her impulses. Approaching the notion of enough with that perspective is empowering and can enhance one's sense of self-worth.

The application of "enough" as a positive tool can create a constructive perspective in many circumstances:

"I've had just enough to eat."

"I've heard enough news."

"I've taken enough time off."

"I've slept enough."

These perspectives require strong self-knowledge, clarity of goals, and personal discipline. Embedded is the mastery of letting go. To walk away from something and say "I've had enough" with a positive and optimistic tone requires us to recognize that although an opportunity might be missed, the advantages of limiting our indulgence in something far outweigh what is given up.

A career plastic surgeon has devoted his life to improving if not saving lives. Focusing on patients' appearance, his skills have helped not just the vanity of aging affluent people, but disfigured and hopeless accident victims. His days have been long and his clients grateful.

Now in his late fifties he pauses to ponder his career. He asks himself, "If I performed one more facelift, would I feel more fulfilled?" Somewhat taken aback by his own voice, he recognizes the truth: "No, I have actually had enough. It is time to do something with even more meaning in my life." That night he pulls out his laptop computer and searches "Doctors Without Borders."

Whether it is how we approach eating, drinking, conversation, diversion, career, or any other form of self-indulgence, walking away and saying "I've had just enough" to ourselves is most motivating. So, the next time you're at a party that hasn't seemed to slow down, and you know you should really get home since the workday is just hours away, be satisfied with the moment and say goodnight.

I've had just enough.

On SELF-TALK

I Did It

WE ALL HAVE ENCOUNTERED INDIVIDUALS WHO ESPOUSE BEING alone—the time to center on their own needs, the ability to focus on making their own decisions, and the simple enjoyment of quiet.

But are things really so silent?

Even when we're not in direct conversation with another, aren't we in constant conversation with ourselves?

That near constant buzz awakens us in the morning: "Ugh, that was a short night."

It accompanies us on our morning commute: "Wow, that guy just cut someone off!"

It is our companion as we decide what to order for lunch: "I had that last week and it wasn't so great."

Some would suggest that such internal communication is just thinking. But its conversational quality might suggest differently.

"I had that last week, and it wasn't so great. But maybe it would be worth trying again. Wait, there's a new item that looks good. OK, I'll order that."

Now, these forms of internal conversation are not deliberate, and they seem to go on all day. They might go on as we sleep at night as well.

But what about more intentional internal conversation—dialogue that is characterized by purposefully talking with oneself, silently or aloud.

We have all tried to have more intentional and directed conversations with ourselves, often engaged in to lessen any negative effects of our own emotions. Perhaps in times of stress, or in simple moments like these:

> At the golf tee: "Hank, now don't look up, bend your knees, and swing through the ball. Relax!"

> Getting ready to go on stage to give a presentation: "Breathe, and talk slowly."

> At the podium to deliver a eulogy: "Help those you are talking to get through this moment. Be a leader. Do not falter."

How effective are these conversations? Do they really help? Possibly. Those who are best at self-talk train themselves, or as with competitive athletes, they are trained to do so. The best athletes develop a ritual of rehearsal before an event. They play and replay scenarios in their mind to bolster their confidence and help manifest their desired results. Do we have to be professional athletes to learn these techniques? Of course not, but we can certainly learn from them.

- **Practice affirmative rituals**: Ritual implies routine, not last minute, seat-of-the-pants, Hail Mary action. The most successful people use ritual to their advantage. Even if it is just saying, "I am OK," enunciated the same way, with the same tone and intentionality, every time. "I'm great. I can do it. I always do my best." Self-centering affirmations, repeated enough to develop into an automatic mantra, can be very effective at improving performance or confidence.

- **Practice anticipation**: As they say, timing is everything. And the same pertains to self-talk. After-the-fact self-care puts us far behind the starting line, whereas preventive care puts us ahead of the curve. Prevention requires anticipation. "I'm going to be meeting with my boss tomorrow for a performance review and compensation discussion. Before I go to bed tonight, after I wake up in the morning, and just before the meeting, I will tell myself, 'I am talented, effective, and worthy' and know it to be true."

Supporting ourselves with consciously directed internal dialogue may seem weak, but in truth it can be far more strengthening than receiving praise from others. If we can't accept others' praise because of our own unconscious negative self-talk, what good does it do us? But if we successfully replace the negative self-talk with positive self-talk, we can then truly say:

"I did it."

On WORDS

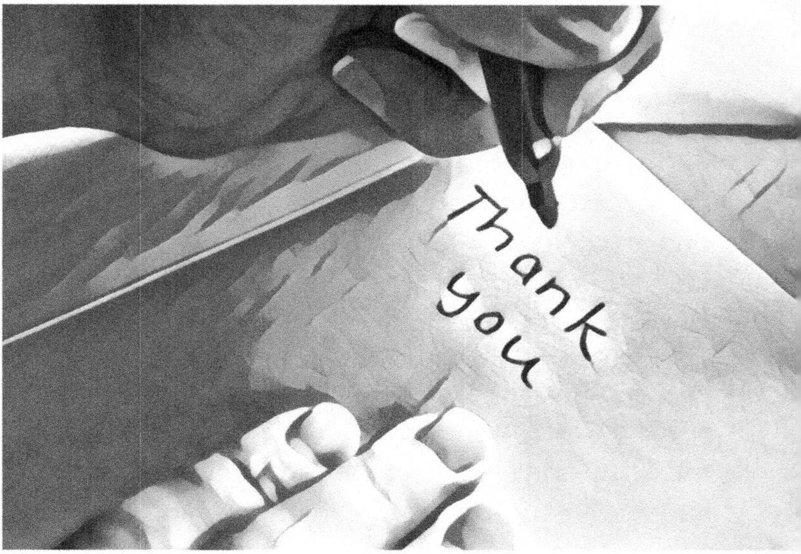
Thank
you

You Are What You Say

GETTING DRESSED FOR AN EVENING EVENT CAN BE STRESSFUL. Cocktail attire, business casual, formal? Colorful, dark, loud? And the never-ending challenge—which shoes? Curiously, a week after the event, most forget the details of their wardrobes and most commonly have no idea what a friend or even a spouse wore.

But let's imagine that at the same event someone mentioned you look "striking" and should "wear that shade more often because it brings out your eye color." That memory would take much longer to fade. More important, if someone critiques another's outfit using the word "dated," those memories may linger forever.

Words contain power. How we use them carries great impact. The specific words we choose in expressing ourselves are certainly more impactful and create a more enduring impression than the appearance we are trying to convey with the very clothes we wear!

We are our words.

Language is complex. The construction of sentences can be challenging. And linking them together into a profound thought or argument may be the essence of effective communication. In truth, individual words are equally important:

- Words alone communicate.

- Words can be permanent.

- Words reflect on the speaker.

Individual words, whether embedded in a complex sentence or pronounced in isolation, have tremendous power. They can be positive and uplifting, or negative and dejecting. They can applaud, or they can criticize. They can be straightforward or nuanced. This cup of coffee is "bitter"; this cup is "weak"; this cup is "cold"; this cup is "terrible." Now this cup is "perfect"!

Depending on the emotional potency of the word and the way it's expressed, it can be permanent. That is, to the listener they can be as perpetual as a nonerasable marker. Words like stupid, ignorant, cute, and short require great care in their use. No less words like smart, efficient, superior, and handsome.

What words convey—not simply about a cup or a person or a situation—includes some insight into the speakers or writers themselves. Some convey eloquence, sensitivity, and education. And others, narrowmindedness, crudeness, and ignorance.

"Have you seen Ellen around recently?"

"Yes, she and I ran into each other at the grocery store." ("She" is a pronoun and is used appropriately.)

"Yes, her and I ran into each other at the tennis court." ("Her" is the possessive pronoun and objective case of "she" and is not used appropriately.)

Which expression says more about a person's worldliness and education? (And if you are confused simply remove "and I" from either sentence to get a sense which sounds correct.)

Admittedly, the use of language and words is changing and does evolve. And someday it may be totally appropriate to say "her and I ran into...," but until then, think before you speak and choose your words carefully. Consider how they affect others. You can't always take them back.

You are what you say.

On
CONVERSATION

Jump In, the Water's Warm

THE PARTY IS CROWDED. HARDLY SPACE TO SQUEEZE THROUGH the room. But not a familiar person in sight. Turn around and leave? There's a good show on TV back home. Go get a drink? Where is the host anyway?

Close by, three people are talking intently. Another person walks up and says, "Hi, I'm Jack. What are we talking about?"

Wow, how did he do that?

Why is conversation so valued?

Why are some people so natural at relating to others?

Can we overcome awkwardness?

How do we keep a conversation going?

To converse is to be human. We thrive on connection—sometimes with shared experiences but most often through conversation. Humans talk about anything and nothing. We share stories; we talk about the world, other people, politics, science, events, and of course, the weather. Conversation can be stimulating, calming, or stressful. But not nearly as stressful as perpetual silence.

Unfortunately, we are not all facile at conversation. There is a real art to contributing to a conversation and keeping it going. It takes observation and reflection. Some seem so natural at talking to others. They enter a conversation deftly. They contribute meaningfully, and they stimulate others to jump in. Often, they tell stories—of just the right length and on just the right topic. But most important, they avoid talking about themselves, ask engaging questions, listen and reflect on what others say.

Jumping into a conversation may seem awkward and threatening. Some may think it best to wait for an invitation. Yet, considering Jack's example, interjecting ourselves into an ongoing dialogue is not antisocial. In fact, it is often embraced. Think back to summers in the backyard when a touch football game was going on. Jumping in and participating was the expectation. Likewise, with others' conversations—even strangers'.

Contributing to a conversation and keeping it going does require some skill. Asking stimulating and occasionally provocative questions can be helpful. Engaging others by asking about themselves and their opinions is vital. Limiting our own opinions is a must. Always seek that balance between speaking and listening. Dominating a conversation will motivate people to find an excuse for a quick exit. Conversation is like rolling snow to make a snowman: too fast and none of the snow sticks; too slow and everyone loses interest. Like a living creature, conversation must be nurtured.

And conversing can feel great! We can...

- Make a valuable connection with someone

- Discover new ideas

- Make new friends

- Evolve future plans

- And grow our self-confidence

So, the next time you enter that room of strangers and are confronted with a sense of intimidation...

Jump in, the water's warm!

On REASONABLE

Perfection Can Be Costly

THE PERFECT WEDDING—AN EVENT THAT MANY PLAN A LIFETIME for. Whoever does the planning, every detail is anticipated and refined over and over. The venue, the attire, the invitation list. It has to be "perfect." And then a grandmother takes ill, the minister is running late, or it rains! Or worse.

Whether it is a wedding or another event, the purchase of a house or a car, or even an entire life, many expect each to be perfect. What is it that drives us to perfection? Wouldn't we all be better off if we simply accepted what was reasonable?

From our youth we are often bred to achieve perfection in so many of our pursuits. When going to religious services, we are dressed as if visiting a queen. We strive to make as many goals as possible in soccer. Students target that perfect "A." As we age the focus evolves to nice attire and of course perfect hair. And for many later in life, the perfect lawn.

Where does this focus on perfection or near perfection get us?

Doesn't it set us up for disappointment?

Or even worse, a sense of personal failure?

A word not spoken enough, but that may result in a much better sense of accomplishment and self-worth, is "reasonable."

Accepting what's reasonable is not without value. In fact, implicit in the word is that we can get across the goal line and that the outcome has worth. And more important, we ourselves have worth in being able to accomplish something that has meaning and satisfaction for us.

Consider the search for a new business location. The options are broad. Purchasing new land and building a facility is at the top of the list. A unique place, custom designed with all the bells and whistles. But is it in the right location? Is it recognizable? Will it draw customers? And of course, the cost!

Then there is that space in a strip mall with quite a bit of foot traffic and many cars driving by. But is it a good fit? Does it clearly speak the brand?

And what about a space in a larger office building? Wouldn't there be more synergy with co-residents, especially if the businesses are complementary or similar? Or would the business get lost in the shuffle?

Decisions such as these can be stressful. Often there are conditions that drive the conclusion, the foremost being money. But that doesn't mean a sense of reasonableness cannot be achieved.

How can we adjust our attitudes to move what's reasonable to the top of our decision paradigm? Consider the following:

- **Recognize**: Perfection may not make us happier. And even if it were achievable, perfection is usually short-lived and rapidly fades.

- **Respect**: Reality awards no winners and losers in life. We all end up in the same place in the long run. Respect that a reasonable outcome may be enough.

- **Revise**: Evaluate your expectations and adjust them accordingly. You could find yourself surprisingly content.

So, the next time you walk into your local sporting goods store looking for the latest state-of-the-art ski jacket, pause for a moment and reflect—the one at home may be just as reasonable. It's possible you might feel good walking out of the store empty handed! And remember:

Perfection can be costly.

On SUCCESS

Forge On

RECENTLY AN ENDURANCE ATHLETE SET OUT TO CROSS THE GREAT continent of Antarctica alone and unassisted—one of the few final frontiers on our planet. The odds were against him; few had ever attempted such a feat, and none had achieved it. The journey was a success, and he will go down in history as a valiant explorer.

There will be receptions in famous places, people to meet, a book to be written, and fame to process. All measures of success?

Success is complex.

> Who defines success?
>
> When do we know we have succeeded?
>
> Is success embedded in the goal or the process?
>
> Are there life ingredients that contribute to success?
>
> If we succeed is our life more complete?

Success: socially or self-defined? Regrettably, much of life's successes are defined by those around us. Early goals of walking and toilet training. Elementary school targets of reading and mastering basic arithmetic. Later in life we may be pushed toward a certain occupation—"How about becoming a doctor?" Whether we like it or not, excess pressure is put on all of us to meet or exceed certain external standards.

Why did that explorer cross Antarctica? For his parents? For future fame? Given his immense effort and sacrifice, his standard of success was likely self-generated. Alone on the ice for days, he could have only had one cause to drive him forward—his own self-motivation and desire to succeed for himself.

What if he had failed? Would he still have been successful? Maybe not in the eyes of the press but perhaps for himself. Only he would know how hard he had pushed himself and whether he had given it his maximal effort. Ultimately, success is a personal standard, one that we self-generate or imbibe and measure internally.

Perhaps the lesson is that success is not measured by whether we reach the goal line, but whether we have focused and exerted enough energy toward achieving the end. What if a goal is too easy to reach? Does that feel like success? And in contrast, falling short but putting it all on the line—isn't that victory?

Success doesn't just happen, although for some it may seem so. What might be some of the ingredients that lead to success?

- **Goals**: A clear objective is an absolute. What is it that must be achieved? What is the end point? Without goals, how can we say we have arrived? And what about the steps along the way? Clarity, again, is a must. Getting more education? Moving to a new location? Assembling a team? Defining way points?

- **Commitment**: Little will happen without personal buy-in. Investment is also an absolute. And yes, some sacrifice may be required. But with the right focus and attitude, pain isn't likely.

- **Encore**: We made it. Is it time to celebrate? Are we now complete? Can we rest on our laurels and bask in their glow? Individual successes are not permanently fulfilling. For many, success begets another goal. After summiting Mt. Everest, Sir Edmund Hillary took the welfare of the Sherpa community to heart and began a successful campaign to raise funds for schools. Jane Goodall, having lived for years in Africa studying gorillas, now at age eighty-five, travels three hundred days a year raising awareness and funds for communities that are central to preserving the treasures of the continent. And personally, I consider my career as a physician a calling, and the work never ends.

Success does not permit rest. Rather than the goal being the end of the journey, it simply begets another. The journey is the success. There is no coasting.

Forge on!

On PROGRESS

Make a Difference—Today

A NEW TRAFFIC LIGHT DOWN THE ROAD. ANOTHER CONSUMER protection law in Congress. Running shoes made of recycled plastic. A cell phone that can perform miracles.

Progress...

Is all progress for the good or is some a step back? Are certain types of progress unnecessary? Is progress something vital? Is progress simply the natural state of the universe? And what of our own personal progress?

Since the beginning of time the world and we as its human inhabitants have been evolving. Our progress for millennia was limited. Although we migrated from Africa through the Middle East to points north and later toward the Pacific, progress as we know it came slowly. Generation after generation living as hunter-gatherers with no sense of agriculture and certainly none of metallurgy. But the pace of change was not to be suppressed forever. We as a species eventually broke through.

Stone to bronze and beyond. Nuts and berries to corn and beyond. The pace of progress accelerated. The renaissance turned attention from religion to humankind. The industrial revolution transformed human labor with the advent of machines. Now, could the information revolution possibly replace human thinking with the likes of "Hal" the computer?

Progress is largely driven by economics. Some may consider that a sad state of affairs, but in truth much of our human interaction with both ourselves and the world is economically based. The exchange of goods and services for another thing of value. Even families function in an economic space.

Edison creates the light bulb, Bell the telephone, and the Wright brothers' the airplane. None of these remarkable additions to our lives would have had any traction had they not also yielded economic gain either directly through sales or indirectly through spin-off products. The printing press, the cotton gin, jet engines, and cell phones. In medicine; penicillin, insulin, CAT scanners, and CRISPR gene editing. Each requires a market. All have an economic upside.

Most progress is intended to better the world. Mass transportation, public education, and social security all appear to add social good. (But what of the copious laws we write in our local, state, and federal legislatures. Well intended, but necessary?) Indoor plumbing, central heating, and the microwave oven all add comfort and convenience.

Conspicuously, not all progress is for the better. While on the surface things may seem to be getting better, below, waves of trouble may brew and often unintended consequences result. Renewable energy displaces the toiling coal miner. The benefits of progress are not uniformly beneficial to all. Some improvements benefit a certain class of our society (those who can afford it) and simultaneously harm the unfortunate. Some progress is in excess and adds little to humankind.

Shouldn't progress be ultimately judged by the value it provides? If only it were so simple. Think of robots that assist in manufacturing.

They may certainly add value to those responsible for manufacturing productivity. They are reliable, they don't complain, and they never go on strike. Again, what of the displaced worker? What of the human toll to that individual? Progress?

Progress, regardless of its value, may therefore be the natural state of the universe. Humans doing what we do best. And yet accepting progress, even if judged valuable and appropriate can be challenging. For it represents change. Changes in thinking, changes in behaviors, changes in routines. Accepting progress and enjoying the experience may be our best response.

In the final analysis, however, progress is really a personal endeavor. Whether outer, such as inventing a solution to one of man's struggles, or inner, including self-improvement and spiritual growth, we are each responsible for our own personal progress. Am I moving forward in life? How can I make today better than yesterday? What can I do to add value to the world? How can I grow in relationship with myself? Consider your own personal progress and...

Make a difference—today.

On FUTURE

Never Out of Sight

THAT TRIP TO YOUR HIGH SCHOOL REUNION IS GETTING CLOSER. Will you remember anyone's name? Recognize the old haunts? Know the way back to your former house? And of course, have you decided what to wear to the gala event? Still months away, but it has been years since your last reunion. Perhaps a slight sense of anxiety mixes with anticipation. Anticipation that will likely grow as the future draws closer.

Looking to the future is powerful!

What purpose does future orientation provide?

Does a future perspective really erode the here and now?

How can we use the future to catalyze our own growth?

How far into the future should we gaze?

Looking to the future is purposeful and can serve us positively. Hope is generated. Plans are made. Creativity is spawned. The heart beats stronger. The mind engages. Thoughts develop. Anticipation draws us forward. All this creates in us a sense of being alive.

Nevertheless, much is made of "living in the moment." For some of us, past orientation or future fixation is our focus—to take us away, consciously or unconsciously, from the here and now, to nullify our authentic selves, to distract us. Yet the future does eventually become this moment. The reunion finally arrives. And your outfit looks great.

Without the future, goals would not be created. Whether it be deadlines or dreams, both are motivating. So the future can be leveraged for our personal growth and gain. Most important, the future portends possibility, and with that, hope. Gazing into the future is potent fuel.

No time in the future is too distant. Next summer. Two years from now. The world our children will inherit. Living on Mars. The planet in 50 years. The planet in 250 years. Thinking deep into the future puts our lives into perspective. Rather than diminishing, it can contribute to a sense that we are part of a greater whole. We are not the end all and be all, but part of a continuous stream of life—and for that we can be grateful.

All we do, all we are, all our intentions serve solely the purpose of the future.

Ours is a human quest of making things better.

Material things, laws, birth of a child, relationships, art, literature—all are created with a vision of the future.

The next time you look in the mirror, consider who you will want to be in five years. If you have children, ask what their lives will be like at your age. Looking up at the moon, think what role it will play in the future of humanity. And as you gaze into the future, remember that vision you are trying to create. A vision to be left...

Never out of sight.

On CHORES

It's All Gotta Be Done!

MANY THINK OF CHORES AS DRUDGERY:

Fold the laundry

Take out the trash

Clean the tub

Lube the car

Clean the gutters

And of course...

Make the bed

Make the bed! Yes, make...the...bed—the paradigm for all chores.

Why do we have chores? Are they simply meaningless tasks? Are they the price we pay for being alive? In spite of their nature of being a nuisance— "What a chore!"—maybe we can acknowledge that chores may add something positive to our lives.

In the military, making the bed is a ritual. Perfect "hospital corners." Tightly drawn enough to bounce a quarter off it. Symmetrical. And rigorously inspected daily. Why is such a mundane activity a ritual?

In the case of soldiers making their beds, a number of life skills are learned. Discipline, rigor, team dynamics, and most important, personal pride.

Our daily chores may in fact provide similar returns for each of us. They add structure to our day, require self-imposed discipline, and in some instances are rewarding. Importantly, they have other attributes:

- Chores are humbling. They keep us aware that few of us are truly entitled.

- Chores connect us with life. They teach us to endure hardship.

- Chores can be rewarding. They provide us a sense of accomplishment.

- Chores can be centering. They put us in touch with ourselves.

To experience these benefits may require us to change our relationship with our chores. We may need to cast off the idea that chores get in the way of what we think of as more important in life. We may need to approach them with acceptance. And optimally we may see them as rewarding.

An older tradesman was working on a home-remodeling project when the owner approached him as he was hunched over, trimming and nailing baseboard along the floor. The owner said, "I'm so sorry this is difficult and not more exciting." To which the laborer replied, "It's all gotta be done."

Correct.

It's all gotta be done!

On NATURE

Look Up

IMAGINE YOURSELF WANDERING ALONG A BEACH. BAREFOOT. EACH step washed by the rhythm of the waves. Coarse, wet sand between the toes. The sun over your shoulder. What thoughts go through your mind?

You are on a wooded trail. It is relatively flat as it winds through a towering forest canopy. It's cool and damp from yesterday's rain. No noise. Just footsteps. Any worries?

Nature. The natural state of things.

> Why is nature important?
>
> What role does nature play in our lives?
>
> Will nature have a role in our future?

Nature, as felt through our toes in the sand or through our breath in a forest, has much personal meaning. For reasons that are profound, when we find ourselves in a natural environment, we connect. A sense of rootedness emerges. Our thoughts often slow. Much that often doesn't make sense seems clearer. Nature is a connector—connecting us both with the environment itself and curiously with ourselves. At the risk of my exploiting a pun, nature grounds us.

We live in such an unnatural world. Artificial light, asphalt pavement, skyscrapers, air conditioning, Gore-Tex, cell phones, board games, electric cars, trains, buses, and planes.

We humans have created an artificial world. Many would claim the benefits of this world in all we have accomplished: increased productivity, enhanced capacity to support an ever-growing population, expanded understanding of the universe, and so on.

From a larger perspective, however, we have not yet and thankfully may never fully separate ourselves from nature. Nature has remained more powerful than us: destructive hurricanes, unmitigated drought, rising sea levels.

Moreover, we are more dependent on nature than we might wish to admit: rain to grow our food and replenish reservoirs, sunlight to energize solar panels, earth's orbit to create seasons, and the moon to fascinate us. In spite of our ingenuity and all that we have created, nature will forever have a role in the existence of humans and all living and inanimate matter.

And in truth we are nature. Carbon, hydrogen, oxygen—the building blocks of all who live come from nature. Building blocks that cycle through our bodies. Nothing permanent. All coming from the environment and returning to the environment. Just as we ultimately will.

As humankind forges a new future with artificial intelligence, robotics, and genetic manipulation, it may become more important than ever to understand our roots. To immerse ourselves in the natural environment around us. To stop and observe. And ultimately to appreciate our place in the universe, keeping us all humble. Perhaps in so doing we will make better judgments, accomplish more with an ethical mindset, and ultimately stay more in touch with ourselves.

Making an effort to connect with nature carries many rewards. Nature settles the soul. It expands our consciousness. Consider activities that just might make that connection, such as simply:

Stepping outside for five minutes.

Taking in your surroundings.

Observing.

Breathing deeply.

Looking at the sky.

Look up. Appreciate.

Look up.

On PLACE

You Are Where You Are

A WORLD-CLASS CORPORATION SEEKS A LOCATION FOR ITS SECOND headquarters. A search committee is organized, and they begin their due diligence. Supply chain access, housing, education, disaster frequency, climate, economic momentum, economic incentives—all duly considered in the committee's work. A large restaurant chain does somewhat the same with a search for their next location—neighborhood socioeconomics, vehicle traffic, work-force availability. Again, all considerations in such critical decision-making.

Each seeking a place. A location. A future.

What really counts?

What makes the most difference?

These corporate decisions are utilitarian. Their choices are profit motivated. Their legacy nil. None will be a Louvre, a Sphinx, a Pantheon, let alone a Yosemite Valley, an Atacama Desert, or a Great Wall.

What really is in a place?

Arguably, many places manifest value that is more than utilitarian. The most iconic are more than the sum of a few characteristics.

Places of the greatest value to us are nodes that orient us not simply to location but to life. They convey direction for humanity itself and serve like a GPS for society at large. They lend meaning to our existence. Yet to achieve this degree of legacy requires transcendent qualities—characteristics that convey more meaning and significance, such as:

Historical events, natural wonders, cultural icons.

And from a human perspective:

Accomplishment, relationship, creativity, and memories.

When taken in aggregate, these characteristics permit place to transcend utility into implicit meaning. Places can express human qualities and accomplishments and social interaction. The Statue of Liberty implies freedom; Chaco Canyon, the origins of North American civilization; Fenway Park, the community of baseball; Fallingwater, human ingenuity; and the local Starbucks, community.

And they depict the unfathomable in nature: immensity in the spectacle of the Grand Canyon, uniqueness in the cactus of Saguaro National Monument, beauty in the red mesas of Monument Valley, and creation in the fauna of the African steppe.

For most of us, place is our home and the community surrounding us. Does it speak to us? Does it have resonance? Do we really feel at home?

Although these questions may seem trivial, they are not. Place affects the spirit. It can be settling and inspiring, or it can be distracting and stultifying.

Ultimately, however, place is what we make of it. The grass will forever appear greener on the other side of the fence. And yet our side of the fence can be made as lush as ever. What values do we want to impute to our place? Even if temporary, each and all characteristics—

style, color, light, hospitableness, safety—create a uniqueness. All say something about us and those we share our lives with.

And let's not forget the final place!

Where will I be buried?

Will it permit closure for my family?

Will it end in destiny?

Does it matter?

But until then, we must deal with the worldly. And for that we must always remember:

You are where you are!

On WEATHER

Today Is Today

IT'S GOING TO RAIN TODAY.

Predicted yesterday. Heard again on the morning wake-up radio, confirmed again by TV news, and once more on the weather app on the car console.

So what?

It's a big deal to many.

> For the commuter listening to a rain forecast: "Should I wear a raincoat or bring an umbrella?"
>
> For the painter: "Do we work outside or in?"
>
> And for the farmer: "Oh no! There is cut hay lying in the field."

But our fascination with the weather can go far beyond the practical. Weather and our moods are seemingly inseparable.

What is weather?

The environment all living creatures exist in contains one vital element—air. And weather seems, simply put, to be the condition of the outside air (a.k.a. the atmosphere) that bathes our bodies and supplies that vital nutrient oxygen to our lungs (and carbon dioxide to plants). How do we describe those conditions? The weather forecaster uses terms we all know: temperature highs and lows, humidity, wind speed and direction, high or low barometric pressure, cloud cover, sunshine, inches of rain, inches of snow, wind chill, tropical depression, hurricane, and so on. The average person uses more common language: hot, humid, cold, breezy, balmy, stifling, invigorating, and depressing.

Some of the imprecise descriptors we use reveal the strong emotional influence of weather. The weather has a daily and uncanny effect on how many of us see the world. Energized? Passive? Optimistic? Gloomy?

Without drawing judgment, you may find it a worthy exercise to observe the influence weather has on your moods. So many of us are excessively focused on the world around us—what other people are doing, the news, the stock market, and of course, the weather. This external focus can be distracting. It can take us away from our inner selves and any sense of serenity or peace within.

Seasonal weather can have even more profound mood-altering consequences. Although principally a sunlight-related effect, seasonal affective disorder can be tragic. Long winter nights aren't simply the source of limited motivation, but can lead to and exacerbate depression. Hence the remarkable suicide rates in Russia and neighboring Baltic countries.

The weather indeed has far-reaching consequences, but none perhaps more profound than global warming. The temperature of the world's atmosphere is definitely rising. Although there may be some controversy surrounding the degree of human activity's contribution to this phenomenon, there is no doubt it is real. The polar ice caps are shrinking, and the oceans are warming. And possibly some weather extremes, such as severe hurricanes, are a consequence. On a human level we are witnessing alarming elevation in urban temperatures, such that cities like Mumbai may someday be uninhabitable. And trends such as these may serve to amplify for all the importance of weather.

In the meantime, the morning forecast for the day: overcast, scattered thunderstorms, and 85 degrees. And I will be happy! For...

Today is today.

On TRAVEL

On the Road Again

Think of your current circumstances. Where are you right now? At a coffee shop preparing for the beginning of the workday? On your daily train commute? In a chair at home letting the evening wind down? Chances are you are at home. But whether you have left or returning, consider your daily routine...

Hear the alarm go off

Let the dog out

Squint in the bright lights of the bathroom

Eat breakfast cereal

Fetch the paper (or open the laptop)

Check messages

Dress for work

Begin the commute

Sound familiar? Sound inspiring?

The odds are good you are not on the road—traveling to some new and invigorating environment. Chances are you are not reading this book waiting in an airport. Chances are very good you are not reading this book on a distant beach.

It's likely, however, that just thinking about these possibilities stirs something. Likely they make the heart pound a bit stronger. Likely they conjure up past adventure.

What about future adventure?

Travel affects us in profound ways, mostly all for the better. It doesn't simply get us out of our comfort zone or our ruts. Travel energizes us. And it is not just the destination.

Travel begins with anticipation. Even a short and perhaps required trip has us planning in advance. Where am I going? What to pack? Passport? Medications? To the airport? Pack the car? House sitter? What about the dog, the cat, or the fish?

More adventuresome excursions amplify the "getting ready." They also begin to stir the soul: My life is in motion. I am going somewhere!

Yes, in travel there is a whole new focus on the self. It is a time of enhanced self-contact. It is often a time of enhanced self-reflection. That companion journal may document all the stops on a voyage, but it may also be filled with deeper thoughts. What should I do with my job—leave or stay? Should I think about moving to a new house? What of the relationship I am leaving behind? How about plans for a new book or a new project? Travel seems to not simply distract us but to draw us forward. This may be the strongest reason to get on the road.

For many, however, travel is daunting. No time. Can't leave the kids. Financially not a good time. I am too old to go through airport security one more time. Are those really meaningful excuses? Do they not just keep us trapped?

Travel doesn't have to be a voyage on the Queen Mary. An afternoon drive to the beach, to the mountains, to a nearby town to shop may suffice. Optimally, it is enough of a sojourn to still require some planning, to tap into the anticipation, and to leave one with a sense of having left town and perhaps experiencing something new. Permitting oneself to step out and really grow is worth all the anxiety and whatever challenges stand as impediments.

Where would you go if you could? To your old hometown? How about your parents' hometowns? A national park? New England in the fall? The Rocky Mountains? Paris? Japan? On an archeology dig? Endless possibilities. No ideas? Pull out a travel magazine and just daydream. Some place will call you.

What would it take to just go? What would it take to be…

On the road again.

Epilogue

On Beginning, Success, Chores, Nature, Travel, . . . is that it? What about Family, Love, Money, Children, Giving, Learning, Art, and Solitude? What about Anger, Acceptance, and Authority? And what about Nothingness, and Death?

These and many more topics represent an endless stream of challenges that we all encounter near daily. They represent waypoints in our journeys, often commanding decision, and action. While a future book may provide the opportunity to address each, perhaps there is no immediate need. Although life's challenges may appear unique, they are in truth very similar. And we all have the capacity to work through them.

As is any journey, waypoints call for a pause. A moment to reflect, and a moment to gather a plan. What is the real issue? Have I experienced that before? How did I previously address this? What would I tell someone in a similar situation? What are my current options? How can I move forward?

Ideally you are now empowered to approach any of life's challenges without intimidation, but with a positiveness of mind. To believe in self-determination and personal capacity. Not to shrink, but to stand tall. For to do so is to be alive!

For those seeking more structure, direction may come from reading and following the exercises detailed in *On LIFE Journal: A Companion Workbook*. The format of this book allows readers to better chart their own courses in life. Not to follow authored recipes but to write their own.

To succeed in engendering such a spirit in those who read these books will be a great reward. For that I will feel that I have completed my task.

Yet another title may remain in order!

It Takes a COMMUNITY

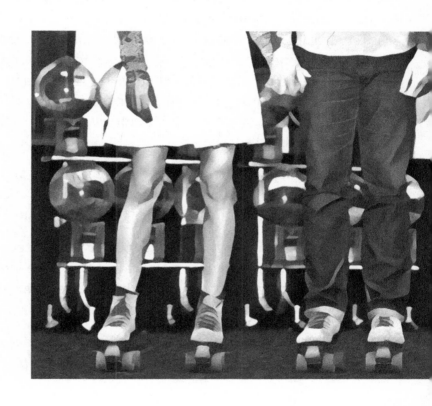

Acknowledgments

A CAREER AS A PHYSICIAN IS FAR FROM STATIC. WHETHER IT BE confronting emergencies and trauma in one's early years, or assisting older individuals to cope with their final days late in one's career, it is a pursuit of constant learning. And for having had that experience I am most grateful. Few have taught me more than my patients—some through sharing their frustrations, others with displays of pure confidence. Their stories are a constant of life lessons to be absorbed.

And as for family, I come from a long line of ministers and mission-aries, whose ethos must have had some unforeseen effect on my understanding of life. For their crusade I am also grateful.

I thank my children, Martha and Haley, whose very presence, though neither would ever say it, has necessitated that I live by example, fueling an ongoing demand to do my best, to seek the most in life, and to be every bit the person I can be.

And finally, my wife, Alice, whose support has permitted my career to flourish and engender the evolution of a well-rounded professional.

$\bullet \ \bullet \ \bullet$

This work would not have come to the page without the help and support of several individuals to whom I give great praise.

My stumbling in a search to find just the right word or phrase to express my thoughts was so helped by Santa Fean Jeff Braucher and his remarkable editing skill. He embraced every concept and assisted with enthusiasm in bringing each to print.

The layout of both this book and its companion journal were the creative efforts of Diane Rigoli of Rigoli Creative (rigolicreative.com). Her energy and added vision made the graphic work stimulating, rewarding, and as much fun as writing. For all her efforts I am indebted.

Our Lifestyle Consultant at Vessel Health, Paige Kinucan, MS, was a companion throughout this adventure. Her expertise in lifestyle medicine along with her life wisdom helped in finalizing many decisions about the book and its layout. Importantly, it is her likeness that can be found in some of the accompanying photo images.

The experience of collaborating with a master photographer was also rich. The photos in this book are the work of Kip Malone, a long-time New Mexico resident. Kip has dedicated himself to recording people's lives, institutional history, and social progress on film for the past 25 years. His engagement for this project included developing an intimate understanding of the subject matter, strategizing on photo representation, critiquing the work product, and assisting in image selection. Kip's other works can be sampled at kipmalone.com. The images included in both the On LIFE book and journal are used with his permission. I am grateful for his contribution and support.

None of this would have happened, however, without the patient guidance of Karen Bomm (iwillpublish.com). Karen devotes herself to assisting budding authors with the process of indie or independent publishing. Her years in the field and knowledge of every element of publishing shine through. She was a tireless champion of my growth as an author and provided support and encouragement throughout the experience. My indebtedness to her is without bounds.

And as Karen says: "It takes a community to build an organization, and it takes the organization's community voice to make a difference."

On the AUTHOR

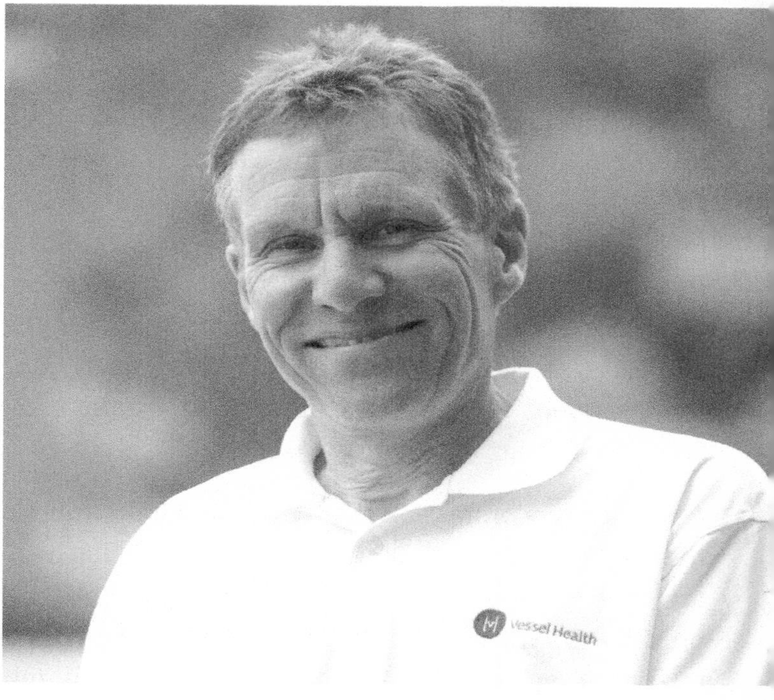
Vessel Health

Harvey J. White, MD, FACC

FOR THE PAST THIRTY-FIVE YEARS DR. WHITE HAS DEDICATED himself to direct patient care, clinical research, and leadership activities designed to improve both individual lives and our healthcare delivery system.

Building on a career in interventional cardiology, including the acute treatment of heart attack and stroke patients, Dr. White is the founder and executive director of Vessel Health, a medical enterprise pioneering prevention in the achievement of cardiovascular well-being. Former developer and medical director of the Heart Hospital of New Mexico, he has served as president of the Greater Albuquerque Medical Association, governor of the American College of Cardiology, president of the American Heart Association, and leader of the Southwest Heart Foundation.

Anchored in a profession that began as a fix-it approach for episodic health challenges, Dr. White has concluded that we, as individuals and as a society, must enhance our focus on prevention and take a proactive approach to maintaining the health of our circulatory system and promoting our personal well-being. Through Vessel Health he supports his commitment to heart health as well as to the health of the greater community. His philosophy in a nutshell: "Treat the system, not the symptom."

A career in cardiology has taught Dr. White that service as a physician entails an appreciation for the breadth of life. He has come to understand that many of our challenges are rooted in broad issues that confront us all. In this book he shares some of the observations he has developed over his years of patient care—and of simply living.

Comments and suggestions are welcome by Dr. White, who can be reached at Guide@OnLifeBook.com.

THERE IS MORE!

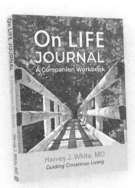

**Did you know that there is a
JOURNAL to accompany this BOOK?**

Titled *On LIFE Journal – A Companion
Workbook*, reading and completing its
encouraging format will bring all the
concepts in On LIFE home. You will find
the exercise stimulating and rewarding!

Learn more about this and
other great thoughts and
ideas on our website at:

VesselPressPublishing.com

Or, to learn more about
Dr. White's novel preventive
health business seek us out at:

Vessel Health
10601 Fourth Street NW
Albuquerque, NM 87114

505-828-3000

VesselNM.com

Made in the USA
Las Vegas, NV
14 May 2021